THE DIS___S
DRIVE

DEVOTIONAL SERIES 2

Dr. Aaron R. Jones

THE DISCIPLE'S DRIVE
Devotional Series 2

Copyright © 2021 by Dr. Aaron R. Jones

Printed in the United States of America

Published by Kingdom Publishing, LLC
Odenton, Maryland

All scripture quotations are from the King James Version of the Bible. Thomas Nelson Publishers, Nashville: Thomas Nelson, Inc. 1972.

Editor: Dr. Sharon D. Jones

Dr. Aaron R. Jones

ISBN: 978-1-947741-68-3

TABLE OF CONTENTS

THE DISCIPLE'S DRIVE

The Disciple's Drive is a devotional series.

The purpose of each series is to encourage every believer to embrace, enhance, and empower his relationship with Jesus Christ. This is one of five series to promote an awareness of one's Christian walk. The ultimate goal is for every believer to be a disciple of Jesus Christ. We, as believers, must be motivated daily to be more like Him; to be His ambassador and to obey His commands. We are to finish this Christian race strong, committed, and determined to complete all God has called us to do.

For the next 21 days, purpose to be driven, like never before, to grow in your walk. Each devotion concludes with a very short prayer, which is meant to be a declaration for that day, and self-assessment questions.

Motivating Factor #1

YOU ARE SPECIAL

Day 1

And be ye kind one to another, tenderhearted, forgiving one another, even as God for Christ's sake hath forgiven you.

Ephesians 4:32

When God created us, He created us to be loved. Desiring love is something God has placed in all of us. This desire for love opens the door for the need to be special in someone's life. Many people search for most of their lives to find that one special person. We fulfill the need to be loved and special in the lives of our children, spouses, church, and community.

In those moments and times when you feel unneeded or unappreciated, trust and know that you are always special to our Heavenly Father. This never changes, because God does not change. He is immutable (Malachi 3:6). We should be grateful to Jesus, not only for the forgiveness of sins, but also for His kindness toward us. We are so special in His sight. Be encouraged, you matter to God!

I am Special!

The Disciple's Prayer Declaration

Dear Lord, thank You for allowing me to be special in Your eyes. Your love, forgiveness, and kindness make me special. Holy Spirit, help me to display this same love, forgiveness, and kindness towards others. In Jesus' Name, Amen.

Can you identify any area(s) of your life that need forgiveness?

_____

_____

_____

_____

_____

What scriptures can you declare to promote forgiveness in those area(s)?

_____

_____

_____

_____

_____

What must you eliminate from your life to allow forgiveness to flow better?

_____

_____

_____

_____

_____

Motivating Factor #2

WALK IN WISDOM

Day 2

But the wisdom that is from above is first pure, then peaceable, gentle, and easy to be intreated, full of mercy and good fruits, without partiality, and without hypocrisy.

James 3:17

James tells us, if we lack wisdom to just ask God (James 1:5). Oftentimes, we are looking for answers and not wisdom. Having the answer may not guarantee that you will understand the problem.

God is the author of wisdom. His wisdom has attributes for us to live a powerful life. When we walk in God's wisdom, our response to people changes. God's wisdom is fruit that produces life changing actions. God's wisdom leads to a sinless life. It creates peace in the atmosphere; and it provides a gentle approach in challenging situations. God's wisdom offers mercy instead of judgment. God's wisdom helps a disciple become who God calls him to be, and not what the world thinks he should be.

I am Wise!

The Disciple's Prayer Declaration

Dear Lord, I do not want to live by my wisdom, but Yours! Please order my steps through Your wisdom and open my ears to hear Your instructions. In Jesus' Name, Amen

Can you identify any area(s) of your life that need wisdom?

_____

_____

_____

_____

_____

What scriptures can you declare to promote wisdom in those area(s)?

_____

_____

_____

_____

_____

What must you eliminate from your life to allow wisdom to flow better?

_____

_____

_____

_____

_____

Motivating Factor #3

STORAGE BIN FOR ETERNITY

Day 3

Laying up in store for themselves a good foundation against the time to come, that they may lay hold on eternal life.

1 Timothy 6:19

We, all, have a lot of things that we have saved to buy homes, cars, tuition, etc. Paul speaks of things we store up for eternity, but they are not material things. Daily, we are making decisions that have eternal implications. Jesus said, *"Lay not up for yourselves treasures upon earth, where moth and rust doth corrupt, and where thieves break through and steal: But lay up for yourselves treasures in heaven, where neither moth nor rust doth corrupt, and where thieves do not break through nor steal"* (Matthew 6:20). Earthly things are temporary in nature, and they will not last forever. They are also first dibs for Satan to corrupt and steal. Disciples of Christ store up prayers, praise, and worship for eternity, and Satan cannot touch them.

I am storing up for Eternity!

The Disciple's Prayer Declaration

Holy Spirit, help my storage bin for eternity to be running over with prayers, praise, and worship unto my Heavenly Father. In Jesus' Name, Amen.

Can you identify any area(s) of your life that need the Storage Bin for Eternity?

_____

_____

_____

_____

_____

What scriptures can you declare to promote kingdom treasures?

_____

_____

_____

_____

What must you eliminate from your life to allow kingdom storing to flow better?

_____

_____

_____

_____

Motivating Factor #4

BEAUTY WITHIN

DAY 4

And if a house be divided against itself, that house cannot stand.

Mark 3:25

The beauty of a home may be the brick, the well-kept yard, the flowers, the carpet, the furniture, the bedrooms, or the size. These things are nice, but real beauty is the unity in a home. Unity in a home brings peace and a loving atmosphere. When there is division in the home, it impacts all of those who live inside.

To keep our homes looking good on the outside, it takes a lot of time and effort. Many people pay to keep their homes looking presentable. As disciples, we are striving to do all that we can to keep the house a home and to maintain the beauty on the inside and outside. A home, as such, is blessed and honored by God. Keep in mind: Outside beauty impresses man, but inside beauty impresses God.

I live in Beauty!

The Disciple's Prayer Declaration

Dear Lord, take up residence in my home and in my family. Unite us together in your Word and presence. Help us to live beautifully within, in Jesus' Name, Amen.

Can you identify any area(s) of your life that need godly beauty?

_____

_____

_____

_____

_____

What scriptures can you declare to promote godly beauty in those area(s)?

_____

_____

_____

_____

_____

What must you eliminate from your life to allow godly beauty to flow better?

_____

_____

_____

_____

Motivating Factor #5

MINDING JESUS' BUSINESS

DAY 5

But seek ye first the kingdom of God, and his righteousness; and all these things shall be added unto you.

Matthew 6:33

Jesus gives us comforting words in this verse. These words are pivotal to how we govern our day. He simply says, "If we take care of His business, then He will take care of ours." Jesus will always provide food, clothing, and shelter. On every to-do-list, we are to embrace Jesus as our number one priority. Our life examples should indicate that Jesus is first.

When we are truly minding the business of the Kingdom, we will focus less on distractions. Let us not just mine our own business, but also mind Jesus' as well. Minding Jesus' business must be as natural as drinking water when your hot; going to bed when you are tired; and driving your car when you need to be somewhere.

I am about Jesus' Business!

The Disciple's Prayer Declaration

Dear Lord, let Your business always be my business. I will put You first in all things. In Jesus' Name, Amen

Can you identify any area(s) of your life that needs to be about Jesus' business?

_____

_____

_____

_____

_____

What scriptures can you declare to promote Jesus' business in those area(s)?

_____

_____

_____

_____

_____

What must you eliminate from your life to allow Jesus' business to flow better?

_____

_____

_____

_____

_____

Motivating Factor #6

CLEAN HEART AND RIGHT WORDS

DAY 6

For with the heart man believeth unto righteousness; and with the mouth confession is made unto salvation.

Romans 10:10

A right heart allows our mouth to say the right things. Jesus said in Matthew 12:34, "… for out of the abundance of the heart the mouth speaketh." The heart makes a connection with our mouth, and it can produce good and evil. Proverbs 18:21 says, "Death and life are in the power of the tongue…"

The Apostle Paul identifies that the heart and the mouth are the connections in our salvation. Our belief (in the heart) which is unto righteousness, through the Holy Spirit, causes us to confess (with our mouths) that Jesus is Lord. The Holy Spirit cleanses our hearts so our mouths will say the right thing.

I have a clean heart!

The Disciple's Prayer Declaration

Dear Lord, search my heart, remove ungodliness, and replace it with your Word. I want to say the right things that will edify people and glorify you. In Jesus' Name, Amen.

Can you identify any area(s) of your life that God needs to work on your heart?

_____

_____

_____

_____

_____

What scriptures can you declare to promote a clean heart and saying right words?

_____

_____

_____

_____

_____

What must you eliminate from your life to allow a cleansed heart to flow better in you?

_____

_____

_____

_____

_____

Motivating Factor #7

BE THANKFUL

DAY 7

In everything give thanks: for this is the will of God in Christ Jesus concerning you.

1 Thessalonians 5:18

It is easy to be thankful when things are falling into place, but it becomes a lot harder when it seems as if life is falling apart. Giving thanks in all things is a needed characteristic for a disciple. When Paul states "in everything," this leaves no room for discussion or doubt. This is the will of God for our lives. Being thankful is a flow in our lives that never stops or retreats. Giving thanks moves forward on good and difficult days. The fact that giving thanks is the will of God, we must make a decision to do it. This decision should be easy, since we serve a faithful, loving, and sovereign God.

I am Thankful!

The Disciple's Prayer Declaration

Dear Lord, this day, my heart, soul, and body praise You for all things, because I know You are in control. In Jesus' Name, Amen

Can you identify any area(s) of your life that you need to be more thankful?

_____

_____

_____

_____

_____

What scriptures can you declare to promote thankfulness in those area(s)?

_____

_____

_____

_____

_____

What must you eliminate from your life to allow thankfulness to flow better?

_____

_____

_____

_____

Motivating Factor #8

DON'T FEAR DEATH, LET DARKNESS FEAR YOU

DAY 8

He will swallow up death in victory; and the Lord GOD will wipe away tears from off all faces; and the rebuke of his people shall he take away from off all the earth: for the LORD hath spoken it.

Isaiah 25:8

In war, one of the biggest weapons is dying. When the fear of dying is gone, the enemy uses it as a weapon against his opponents. He will do anything to obtain victory, even if it costs his own life.

As disciples, once the fear of death is conquered, then we are able to walk through the dark valleys of life. God, through Jesus, defeated death. Death no longer has a hold on our lives. Satan should not be able to shake Death in our faces, and we fear it. We are victorious over Death.

I am Victorious!

The Disciple's Prayer Declaration

Dear Lord, keep me strong in You, so death will not have any hold on me. In Jesus' Name, Amen

Can you identify any area(s) of your life that you need to conquer the fear of death?

_____

_____

_____

_____

_____

What scriptures can you declare to promote light and life in those area(s)?

_____

_____

_____

_____

_____

What must you eliminate from your life to allow light and life to flow better?

_____

_____

_____

_____

_____

Motivating Factor #9

TOP SHELF OFFERING

DAY 9

And if ye offer the blind for sacrifice, is it not evil? and if ye offer the lame and sick, is it not evil? offer it now unto thy governor; will he be pleased with thee, or accept thy person? saith the LORD of hosts.

Malachi 1:8

We learn from the story of Cain and Abel that God doesn't take pleasure in all offerings. "*And Abel, he also brought of the firstlings of his flock and of the fat thereof. And the LORD had respect unto Abel and to his offering: But unto Cain and to his offering he had not respect*" (Genesis 4:4,5). It was not just the sacrifice, but the heart of the sacrifice.

God's children had their hearts in the wrong place, so they gave lame and blind offerings. Our giving is more about what is in our hearts rather than what is in our hands. Every time we give to God, He is looking at our hearts. When our heart is in the right place, we give God a top shelf offering every time.

I will give God Top Shelf Offerings!

The Disciple's Prayer Declaration

Dear Lord, I will give you the best and not the least! In Jesus' Name, Amen

Can you identify any area(s) of your life that you are not giving God your best?

_____

_____

_____

_____

_____

What scriptures can you declare to promote better giving in those area(s)?

_____

_____

_____

_____

_____

What must you eliminate from your life to allow giving to flow better?

_____

_____

_____

_____

_____

Motivating Factor #10

REJOICE AND WEEP

DAY 10

Rejoice with them that do rejoice, and weep with them that weep.

Romans 12:15

We should support one another through the joyous and challenging moments of life. Sometimes it may be difficult, because the range of emotions can be endless.

I believe we are called to fill that specific role in the life of certain people. We have to be careful not to take on every person we come in contact with. God has not called us to rescue everyone, but according to His divine plan, He has outlined the lives you should impact. We must be sensitive to the Holy Spirit. We should reframe putting unneeded pressure on ourselves, if we cannot be there for everyone at all times. We are not God! Let's not beat ourselves up. God will guide us in the right direction, and He will have us there at the right time.

I am balanced in my rejoicing and weeping!

The Disciple's Prayer Declaration

Dear Lord, please lead me to the people You want me to encourage and celebrate Your blessings in their lives. In Jesus' Name, Amen

Can you identify any area(s) of your life that needs balance in rejoicing and weeping with others?

_____

_____

_____

_____

_____

What scriptures can you declare to promote the balance of rejoicing and weeping in those area(s)?

_____

_____

_____

_____

_____

What must you eliminate from your life to allow rejoicing and weeping to flow better?

_____

_____

_____

_____

_____

Motivating Factor #11

DELIGHTING IN GOD'S WORD

DAY 11

*Blessed art thou, O LORD: teach me thy statutes.
With my lips have I declared all the judgments
of thy mouth. I have rejoiced in the way of
thy testimonies, as much as in all riches. I will
meditate in thy precepts, and have respect unto
thy ways. I will delight myself in thy statutes: I
will not forget thy word.*

Psalm 119:12-16

The Psalm writer gives an incredible approach
to God's Word. First, he asked to be taught
the Word. Secondly, he will declare the Word.
Thirdly, he will rejoice in the Word. Fourthly, he
will meditate on the Word. Fifthly, he will delight
in the word. Finally, he will not forget the Word.

The Word of God is meant to teach, transform,
bless, guide, and correct us. We see in our
passage, there is a godly responsibility we have
to the Word of God.

When we hear God's Word, we should respond by
declaring; rejoicing; meditating; delighting; and
holding it close in our hearts. I believe delighting
is the key to them all. Having a genuine joy for

the Word will lead to the other three. God's Word is more than a Means to a blessing, but a Methodology for discipleship living.

I have Joy because God's Word!

The Disciple's Prayer Declaration

Dear Lord, as I go deeper into Your Word, let my desire to delight in it grow stronger each day. In Jesus' Name, Amen

Can you identify any area(s) of your life that needs more of God's Word?

_____

_____

_____

_____

_____

What scriptures can you declare to promote a greater desire for God's Word in those area(s)?

_____

_____

_____

_____

_____

What must you eliminate from your life to allow God's Word to flow better?

_____

_____

_____

_____

_____

Motivating Factor #12

YOUR BUILDING IS NOT
FOR YOU

DAY 12

Furthermore David the king said unto all the congregation, Solomon my son, whom alone God hath chosen, is yet young and tender, and the work is great: for the palace is not for man, but for the LORD God.

1 Chronicles 29:1

When build something, we gain a sense of accomplishment. Building is important in life. What God allows us to build is not for us, but ultimately for His glory. God getting the glory is what makes the work great.

When we build just for our own recognition, it is a vain work. Solomon says, *"Except the LORD build the house, they labour in vain that build it (Psalm 127:1)."* Disciples build the kingdom of God out of obedience to the Word of God. This allows God's name to be glorified throughout the earth.

Let us build not to Brag on us, but to Boast on God!

The Disciple's Prayer Declaration

Dear Lord, cause me to always keep your glory in my view, and that everything I build lifts Your Name on high. In Jesus' Name, Amen

Can you identify any area(s) of your life where you are not building for God?

_____

_____

_____

_____

_____

What scriptures can you declare to promote kingdom building glory in those area(s)?

_____

_____

_____

_____

_____

What must you eliminate from your life to allow God's glory to flow better?

_____

_____

_____

_____

_____

Motivating Factor #13

SACRIFICES GO A LONG WAY

DAY 13

Hereby perceive we the love of God, because he laid down his life for us: and we ought to lay down our lives for the brethren.

1 John 3:16

Discipleship living is about love and sacrifices. When we love sacrificing for others, it becomes something that we do. Love will have us move our schedule around, go out our way, and do things that are not on the top our list.

Sometimes it is the small sacrifices that shows the love we have for someone. We sacrifice, because Jesus sacrificed. Sacrificing for one another should be a way of life. There are many who appreciate hearing the words "I Love You," but the completion of the statement is that love is sacrificial.

Love is a Tell and Take. Tell them you love them, and Take the time to show them.

I am giving more than just words, but my actions!

The Disciple's Prayer Declaration

Dear Lord, teach me to love in word and indeed.
In Jesus' Name, Amen

Can you identify any area(s) of your life where you need to show sacrificial love?

_____

_____

_____

_____

_____

What scriptures can you declare to promote sacrificial love in those area(s)?

_____

_____

_____

_____

What must you eliminate from your life to allow sacrificial love to flow better?

_____

_____

_____

_____

Motivating Factor #14

NEVER WAVE
THE WHITE FLAG

DAY 14

But thou, O man of God, flee these things; and follow after righteousness, godliness, faith, love, patience, meekness.
Fight the good fight of faith, lay hold on eternal life, whereunto thou art also called, and hast professed a good profession before many witnesses.

1 Timothy 6:11, 12

We were never promised that this Walk of Faith would be easy. We are promised that God would never leave nor forsake us (Hebrews 14:5). The Apostle Paul does not tell us to stay in the fight with superficial initiatives, but he encourages us to follow righteousness, godliness, faith, love, patience, and meekness. These characteristics prepare us for the fight and keeps us strong during the fight.

I encourage you today, don't WAVE a White Flag to surrender or negotiate with Satan, but WAIT on the Blood-stained banner. The hymn says, *"The Blood that gives me strength from day to day. It will never lose its power."*

Don't Give Up, Keep Fighting the Good Fight of Faith!

The Disciple's Prayer Declaration

Dear Lord, help me not to wave the white flag!
Keep me in this fight of life and ministry. I yield
myself to You. In Jesus' Name, Amen

Can you identify any area(s) of your life where you need to keep fighting?

_____

_____

_____

_____

_____

What scriptures can you declare to promote fighting and not surrendering in those area(s)?

_____

_____

_____

_____

_____

What must you eliminate from your life to allow the fight flow better?

_____

_____

_____

_____

_____

Motivating Factor #15

NOT MY WILL

DAY 15

And this is the confidence that we have in him, that, if we ask any thing according to his will, he heareth us: And if we know that he hear us, whatsoever we ask, we know that we have the petitions that we desired of him.

I John 5:14, 15

Disciples of Jesus Christ understand that their prayers are not a blank check to God. Our prayer closet is where we can hear from God and speak to Him. We want these moments to be filled with the Presence of the Holy Spirit. Praying in the will of God should be the ultimate desire of a disciple's prayer life. Our prayer requests should be aligned with God's will for our lives, family, church, and community. God's Word is His will. God is not obligated to pursue our own plans and personal agenda. God will hasten to His Word to perform it (Jeremiah 1:12).

I want Your Will!

The Disciple's Prayer Declaration

Dear Lord, help me to always seek only Your will for my life. I do not want my will, but God's will to be done. In Jesus' Name, Amen.

Can you identify any area(s) of your life that needs the clarity of God's will?

_____

_____

_____

_____

What scriptures can you declare to promote God's will in those area(s)?

_____

_____

_____

_____

What must you eliminate from your life to allow God's will to flow better?

_____

_____

_____

_____

Motivating Factor #16

NOT FOR MY FAME, BUT FOR YOUR NAME

DAY 16

But do thou for me, O GOD the Lord, for thy name's sake: because thy mercy is good, deliver thou me.

Psalm 109:21

When God intervenes in our lives, we are beneficiaries of His sovereignty. It is the sovereignty of God that brings us under subjection. Our deliverance from the hands of Satan is made possible through the omnipotence of God.

David wanted personal deliverance, but he declared it to be done for the Lord's name sake. Our deliverance will draw people to Jesus. It may make us look and feel better. It will make us an asset to the Kingdom of God. Overall, it is done for God to get the glory.

David says in Psalm 23:3, "He restoreth my soul: He leadeth me in the paths of righteousness for His name's sake."

Not for my Fame, but for your Name!

The Disciple's Prayer Declaration

Dear Lord, let Your name be glorified through my deliverance. In Jesus' Name, Amen

Can you identify any area(s) of your life that needs the identity of Jesus?

_____

_____

_____

_____

_____

What scriptures can you declare to promote Jesus' name in those area(s)?

_____

_____

_____

_____

_____

What must you eliminate from your life to allow the name of Jesus to flow better?

_____

_____

_____

_____

Motivating Factor #17

WALKING
CIRCUMSPECTLY

DAY 17

*See then that ye walk circumspectly, not as fools,
but as wise, Redeeming the time, because the
days are evil. Wherefore be ye not unwise, but
understanding what the will of the Lord is.*

Ephesians 5:15-17

Believers never go to sleep. This doesn't mean we
don't go to bed, close our eyes, and rest. It means
we are always conscious that Jesus can return
at any moment. So, there is not a day where we
walk in ignorance or walk unwise. Wise disciples
live their lives in awareness of Jesus' coming.
This awareness guides our daily activities. We
understand there is no time to waste; and the
will of God is of the utmost priority in our lives.
The days are not going to get better, so we must
keep battling.

Jesus makes it clear that the day and hour
knoweth no man, no, not the angels of heaven,
but my Father only (Matthew 24:36).

Stay Awake! Walk Alert!

The Disciple's Prayer Declaration

Dear Lord, teach us to walk circumspectly and to redeem time, not waste it. In Jesus' Name, Amen

Can you identify any area(s) of your life where you need to walk circumspectly?

_____

_____

_____

_____

_____

What scriptures can you declare to promote circumspective walking in those area(s)?

_____

_____

_____

_____

_____

What must you eliminate from your life to allow walking circumspectly to flow better?

_____

_____

_____

_____

_____

Motivating Factor #18

FOCUS ON THE UNSEEN

DAY 18

But his delight is in the law of the LORD; and in his law doth he meditate day and night. And he shall be like a tree planted by the rivers of water, that bringeth forth his fruit in his season; his leaf also shall not wither; and whatsoever he doeth shall prosper.

Psalm 1:2, 3

The root is the part of the tree that is not seen. They say it is the most important part of the tree. The roots provide the necessary nutrients for the tree itself; without it, the tree would not receive nourishment or water.

People see the gifts and fruit in our lives, but they never see the study, meditation, and time spent with the Lord. This is the unseen part that makes us strong. Discipleship living embraces the unseen part more than the seen. When we reverse this principle, our walk becomes more of a show than a true sacrifice to God.

Strong Roots produce Strong Results!

The Disciple's Prayer Declaration

Dear Lord, keep my focus on the unseen, so that You will get the glory in the seen. In Jesus' Name, Amen

Can you identify any area(s) of your life that need stronger roots in God?

_____

_____

_____

_____

_____

What scriptures can you declare to promote the development of stronger roots in those area(s)?

_____

_____

_____

_____

_____

What must you eliminate from your life to allow stronger roots to flow better?

_____

_____

_____

_____

_____

Motivating Factor #19

T. L. C.

DAY 19

Let nothing be done through strife or vainglory;
but in lowliness of mind let each esteem other
better than themselves.

Philippians 2:3

Maturity as a disciple is shown when we can honor our brothers and sisters in the Lord. Oftentimes when we see people, we cannot see what they are going through in their personal lives. If we knew half of a person's story, it probably would blow our minds. We all need a push to make it through life's challenging days.

Paul teaches us how to brighten someone's day. He uses the word esteem, which simply means to respect or to admire someone. More importantly, Paul encourages us to esteem others better than ourselves. It is important that disciples know to give some T.L.C.: Treat people with respect. Listen to their struggle. Clap for their accomplishments.

Do you need some T.L.C.?

The Disciple's Prayer Declaration

Dear Lord, help me to give T.L.C. to people. Help me to find the good in those I encounter. Teach me to esteem others above myself.
In Jesus' Name, Amen

Can you identify any area(s) of your life that need T.L.C.?

_____

_____

_____

_____

_____

What scriptures can you declare to promote T.L.C. in those area(s)?

_____

_____

_____

_____

_____

What must you eliminate from your life to allow T.L.C. to flow better?

_____

_____

_____

_____

_____

Motivating Factor #20

GOD STANDS ALONE

DAY 20

Fear ye not, neither be afraid: have not I told thee from that time, and have declared it? ye are even my witnesses. Is there a God beside me? yea, there is no God; I know not any.

Isaiah 44:8

Our God stands alone! He is above any other assumed gods. There is no god that compares to the only Triune God (God the Father, God the Son, and God the Holy Spirit). The gods of the Old Testament had to be designed and developed by a man. In verse 6, God makes known that He is the first and the last.

God is eternal and self-existent. He doesn't need anything to allow Him to exist. Isaiah makes known that we are witnesses to the sovereignty of God. We are challenged to declare the mighty power of God in our lives. What should encourage us not to walk in fear or to desire to create an object god is knowing that we serve the only True God. The release of fear and idol worship is knowing who God is, and who I am in Him.

Walking with My God!

The Disciple's Prayer Declaration

Dear Lord, allow me to never doubt who You are, and who You are in me. Strengthen me to always walk in faith and not fear. In Jesus' Name, Amen

Can you identify any area(s) of your life that needs release from fear?

_____

_____

_____

_____

_____

What scriptures can you declare to promote faith in those area(s)?

_____

_____

_____

_____

_____

What must you eliminate from your life to allow faith in God to flow better ?

_____

_____

_____

_____

_____

Motivating Factor #21

PRAYER BEFORE PLANNING

DAY 21

*And Jacob said, O God of my father Abraham,
and God of my father Isaac, the LORD which
saidst unto me, Return unto thy country, and to
thy kindred, and I will deal well with thee:*

Genesis 32:9

Jacob was afraid to meet his brother, Esau, after his deception in stealing his blessings. Jacob's past behaviors convinced him to make plans (if Esau decides to war with him). God had already showed Himself to Jacob. God showed Jacob that He would be with him. Verse 1 says, "And Jacob went on his way, and the angels of God met him." After Jacob puts his plan in place, then he prays to God.

It is easy to allow our emotions to make us go ahead of God, as if we have a better solution. Jacob let his emotions get the best of him, then he realized that God was the one that sent him to his destination. Therefore, God was the one to protect him. Disciples must remember to pray to God before planning, not the reverse.

Pray before Planning!!!

The Disciple's Prayer Declaration

Dear Lord, teach me not to go ahead of You.
When situations arises, I will seek Your face first.
In Jesus' Name, Amen

Can you identify any area(s) of your life that need more praying and less planning?

_____

_____

_____

_____

_____

What scriptures can you declare to promote more prayer in those area(s)?

_____

_____

_____

_____

_____

What must you eliminate from your life to allow prayer to flow better?

_____

_____

_____

_____

_____

About the Author

Dr. Aaron R. Jones serves as Senior Pastor of New Hope Church of God of Waldorf, Inc. and New Hope COG World Missions. He is the Executive Director of New Hope Community Outreach Services, Inc.

Dr. Jones serves the Church of God's Delmarva-DC Region as Coordinator of the Ministerial Internship Program; Chairman of the Intercultural Advisory Committee; Member of the World Missions Board; and Chaplain's Board. In his local community, Dr. Jones serves as a Chief of Chaplains for the Charles County Sheriff's Office; Board Secretary for the United Ministers Coalition of Southern Maryland, Inc.; Board Member of the VConnections in Waldorf, MD; Co-Chair of Religious Affairs Committee of the Charles County NAACP; a Community Mediator for Charles County; and Board Chairman for the City of Refuge Baltimore.

Dr. Jones received a Doctorate in Theology and Pastoral Counseling from Life Christian University and a Doctorate in Christian Counseling from American Christian College and Seminary. He is a Certified Pastoral Counselor with the International Association of Christian Counseling Professionals. He is an Associate Certified Coach with the International Coach Federation.

Dr. Jones is the founder and owner of God's Comfort Ministries. He has published 37 books/workbooks, a soul-winning project, and an evangelism and discipleship training program. He has recorded two CDs. Dr. Jones has been a featured guest on four national TV shows, two radio broadcast shows, and two Christian magazines.

Dr. Jones served over 20 years in the Armed Forces. He is a retired Army Chaplain. He participated in both Operation Noble Eagle (2003) and Operation Iraqi Freedom III (2005). Dr. Jones is happily married to his wife, Sharon, for 24 years.

CPSIA information can be obtained
at www.ICGtesting.com
Printed in the USA
BVHW041000080921
616302BV00018B/441